D0646271

# BASKETBALL IN THE
# SEC
## (SOUTHEASTERN CONFERENCE)

rosen publishing's
**rosen central**®

New York

**GREG ROZA**

*For Christine, Marcus, and Juliet*

Published in 2008 by The Rosen Publishing Group, Inc.
29 East 21st Street, New York, NY 10010

First Edition

**Library of Congress Cataloging-in-Publication Data**

Roza, Greg.
Basketball in the SEC (Southeastern Conference) / Greg Roza. — 1st ed.
      p. cm. — (Inside men's college basketball)
Includes bibliographical references and index.
ISBN-13: 978-1-4042-1382-1 (lib. bdg.)
1. Southeastern Conference. 2. Basketball—Southern States. I. Title.
GV885.415.S68R69 2008
796.323'630973—dc22

2007028259

*Manufactured in the United States of America*

**On the cover:** *(Top)* The Kentucky bench watches action on the court during the 2006 SEC Men's Basketball Tournament. *(Bottom)* Tennessee Volunteer Jordan Howell (15) looks on as Florida Gator Al Horford (42) dunks for a basket during the first half of a February 2007 game. The Gators went on to win, 94–78.

# CONTENTS

# INTRODUCTION

**The** Southeastern Conference (SEC) basketball teams have been battling on the court since the late 1800s. In a conference known for outstanding football, SEC basketball has stolen much of the college sports' spotlight in the past decade. The conference, which has existed in its current form since 1992, has been one of the most dominant conferences in the NCAA (National Collegiate Athletic Association).

SEC basketball teams are a common sight in the postseason. All twelve teams have made it to the NCAA tournament at least once since 2002. Several SEC teams have been particularly outstanding. Kentucky has won forty-three SEC championships, twenty-four SEC tournament titles, and seven national championships. Alabama has six SEC tournament titles. Florida, the most

On January 24, 2007, the Georgia Bulldogs defeated the Kentucky Wildcats 78–69 in front of a sold-out crowd at Stegeman Coliseum. The Athens, Georgia, stadium was named in honor of Herman Stegeman, who coached basketball and other sports at the University of Georgia from 1919 to 1939.

recent success story, won back-to-back national championships in 2006 and 2007.

In 2006, SEC teams Florida and South Carolina, respectively, won the NCAA tournament and the NIT (National Invitation Tournament). Out of the thirty-one men's basketball conferences, it is one of only four to accomplish this feat. In 2007, the SEC became the first conference to win three national championships in one year: men's basketball (Florida), women's basketball (Tennessee), and football (Florida). Florida is the only school besides the University of Connecticut to win both the men's and women's basketball national championships in the same year. Additionally, Florida is the only team to win both basketball and football championships in the same year. With results like these, it is easy to see why many fans, coaches, and experts consider the SEC to be the premier conference in college sports.

# The History of Basketball and the SEC

**James** Naismith, a physical-education instructor, invented basketball in 1891. Within ten years, basketball was being played in hundreds of YMCAs (Young Men's Christian Associations) and colleges. In its early years, some of the sport's most notable characteristics—such as backboards, free throws, the three-point shot, and dribbling the ball—had not yet been established. As Naismith's game became more popular over time, however, it came to resemble the sport with which we are familiar today.

In 1892, Geneva College in Beaver Falls, Pennsylvania, was the first college to form a basketball team. Many other colleges around the country quickly followed suit. In 1893, Vanderbilt University was the first SEC school to start a basketball program. Its team played games at the Nashville YMCA. Although the makeup of the SEC has changed several times throughout the last century and has included dozens of teams, the conference has always shown a

The above collection of items related to Dr. James Naismith was up for auction in 2006. Naismith is shown in the photo on the right, and the photo on the left shows his first basketball team. Below the photos are game diagrams drawn by Naismith and one of his whistles.

dominant presence on the court. The SEC's current structure of twelve teams, divided into East and West Divisions, has existed since 1992.

## The SIAA

Although the Southeastern Conference did not actually form until 1932, its history can be traced back to the 1890s. In 1894, Dr. William Dudley, a chemistry professor at Vanderbilt College, initiated a movement to organize the first collegiate athletic conference in the United States. On December 22, 1894, representatives from seven southeastern schools met in Atlanta, Georgia, to discuss the future of collegiate sports in their area of the country. They formed the Southern Intercollegiate Athletic Association (SIAA). The original SIAA members were the University of Alabama, Alabama Polytechnic Institute (which became Auburn University in 1960), the University of Georgia, Georgia School of Technology (known as Georgia Tech), the University of North Carolina, the University of the South (known as Sewanee), and Vanderbilt University. The next year, nineteen other schools joined the SIAA.

At this time, basketball rules and regulations were not consistent from school to school. Courts, for example, were often different

## James Naismith and the Birth of Basketball

James Naismith was born in Canada, near Almonte, Ontario, on November 6, 1861. After graduating from Montreal's McGill University in 1887, Naismith became an instructor at the YMCA Training School in Springfield, Massachusetts. In 1891, the director of the school challenged the instructors to come up with a regimen of exercise that would keep students busy in the time between the football and baseball seasons. Naismith devised a sport that could be played indoors with little equipment. It proved to be the perfect activity to keep teenage students busy and interested in physical activity. In 1892, Naismith published the original thirteen rules of basketball in the Springfield College newspaper, the *Triangle*. His students took their knowledge of the game home with them and played it in their local YMCAs.

Basketball soon became popular throughout the United States and Canada. It quickly spread to other countries as well. Naismith continued to develop the game and helped to establish a basketball association. In 1898, he became a professor at the University of Kansas and the school's first basketball coach. Several of the sport's most memorable coaches learned from Naismith, particularly Forrest "Phog" Allen, who became known as the father of basketball coaching.

Basketball officially became an Olympic sport during the 1936 Olympic Games in Berlin, Germany. Naismith handed out medals to the winning teams. While at the Olympics, he was also named the honorary president of the International Basketball Federation (FIBA).

sizes depending on the school. Some courts even contained columns or other obstructions. Differences like this often gave home teams the advantage. The teams that played the most games at home often won the most games.

By 1920, the SIAA stretched from Maryland to Texas and had a total of thirty schools. The larger the conference became, the more problems arose. Its smaller and larger schools generally did not

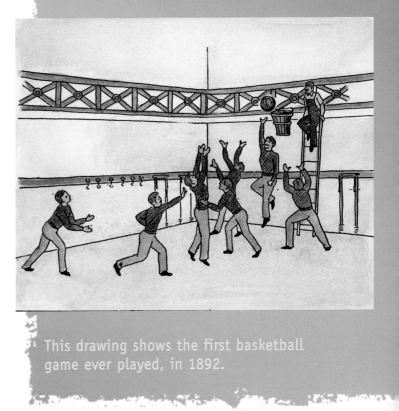

This drawing shows the first basketball game ever played, in 1892.

agree about allowing freshmen to play on their main teams. The disagreements eventually led to the breakup of the SIAA. At a meeting in Gainesville, Florida, on December 12 and 13, 1920, fourteen of the larger SIAA schools split off to form the Southern Conference (SC). The rest of the SIAA eventually broke up to form other conferences.

## The SC

Initially, the Southern Conference was made up of fourteen schools: Alabama, Auburn, Clemson, Georgia, Georgia Tech, Kentucky, Maryland, Mississippi State, North Carolina, North Carolina State, Tennessee, Virginia, Virginia Tech, and Washington and Lee. The popularity of basketball and other college sports grew quickly throughout the early 1900s. Therefore, the SC grew as well. In 1922, seven more schools joined the conference: Florida, Louisiana State University

| | SCHOOL | TEAM NAME | YEAR JOINED SEC | SEC REGULAR SEASON CONFERENCE CHAMPLIONSHIPS | SEC TOURNAMENT TITLES | NCAA TOURNAMENT APPEARANCES |
|---|---|---|---|---|---|---|
| **EASTERN DIVISION** | University of Florida | Gators | 1932 | 4 | 3 | 14 |
| | University of Georgia | Bulldogs | 1932 | 1 | 1 | 9 |
| | University of Kentucky | Wildcats | 1932 | 43 | 25 | 47 |
| | University of South Carolina | Gamecocks | 1992 | 1 | 0 | 8 |
| | University of Tennessee | Volunteers | 1932 | 8 | 4 | 15 |
| | Vanderbilt University | Commodores | 1932 | 3 | 1 | 9 |
| **WESTERN DIVISION** | University of Alabama | Crimson Tide | 1932 | 7 | 6 | 19 |
| | University of Arkansas | Razorbacks (Hogs) | 1992 | 2 | 1 | 29 |
| | Auburn University | Tigers | 1932 | 2 | 1 | 8 |
| | Louisiana State University (LSU) | Tigers | 1932 | 9 | 1 | 19 |
| | University of Mississippi | Ole Miss Rebels | 1932 | 0 | 1 | 6 |
| | Mississippi State University | Bulldogs | 1932 | 6 | 2 | 8 |

(LSU), Mississippi, South Carolina, Tulane, Vanderbilt, and Virginia Military. Sewanee joined in 1923, and Duke became a member in 1928. The total number of SC schools was up to twenty-three. Soon, the conference began to face problems similar to those that the SIAA had faced just ten years earlier. Arguments over recruiting concerns, academic standards, and team travel caused further problems.

The Southern Conference decided that it had once again become too large. In 1932 in Knoxville, Tennessee, SC representatives divided the conference in two. The ten schools along the Atlantic Coast stayed in the Southern Conference. The remaining thirteen formed the Southeastern Conference, or SEC.

| NCAA TOURNAMENT WIN/LOSS (winning percentage) | NCAA FINAL FOUR APPEARANCES | NCAA CHAMPIONSHIPS | SEC CONFERENCE PLAYERS OF THE YEAR | FIRST-ROUND NBA DRAFT PICKS |
|---|---|---|---|---|
| 27–12 (.692) | 4 | 2 | 0 | 9 |
| 7–9 (.438) | 1 | 0 | 1 | 6 |
| 98–43 (.695) | 13 | 7 | 12 | 20 |
| 4–9 (.308) | 0 | 0 | 0 | 8 |
| 11–15 (.423) | 0 | 0 | 10 | 7 |
| 9–9 (.500) | 0 | 0 | 6 | 3 |
| 20–19 (.513) | 0 | 0 | 5 | 14 |
| 39–28 (.582) | 6 | 1 | 2 | 11 |
| 12–8 (.600) | 0 | 0 | 2 | 6 |
| 23–22 (.511) | 4 | 1 | 10 | 12 |
| 3–6 (.333) | 0 | 0 | 2 | 1 |
| 10–8 (.556) | 1 | 0 | 6 | 6 |

# The SEC

The original thirteen schools in the SEC were Alabama, Auburn, Florida, Georgia, Georgia Tech, Kentucky, LSU, Mississippi, Mississippi State, Sewanee, Tennessee, Tulane, and Vanderbilt.

In 1940, Sewanee opted to focus more on academics than on athletics and left to become a Division III school. Georgia Tech joined the Atlantic Division Conference in 1964. In 1966, Tulane joined Conference USA. The SEC remained at ten schools until 1992, when Arkansas and South Carolina joined. This brought the total number of SEC schools to twelve, and it was divided into East and West Divisions.

# 2 CHAPTER

# Key Coaches in the SEC

**The** SEC has been home to some of the best coaches in the history of college basketball. Some of the first coaches in the SEC helped to shape the way the game is played today, and some even learned from James Naismith. The tradition of great coaching has continued throughout the twentieth century with brilliant leaders such as Rick Pitino, who led the Kentucky Wildcats to the national championship in 1989. At the University of Florida, Billy Donovan is currently the head coach. Since joining the Gators in 1996, Donovan has changed a losing team into the best team in college basketball—and he has two national championships to prove it.

## Adolph Rupp

Adolph Rupp was the Kentucky Wildcats' coach from 1930 until he retired in 1972. Among his many achievements, in forty-one seasons,

This picture of coach Adolph Rupp *(left)* and the Kentucky Wildcats was taken before a game with Xavier University in 1954. Rupp and the team were presented with a cake celebrating eleven years without a defeat at home. The Wildcats won 115 straight home games.

Rupp won 879 games. This is the third-best record ever for a college basketball coach.

As a student at the University of Kansas from 1919 to 1923, Rupp played on the basketball team. This gave him the opportunity to learn all he could about coaching from two basketball legends: Coach Forrest "Phog" Allen—known as the father of basketball coaching—and James Naismith, the man who invented the sport.

After graduating from Kansas, Rupp became a high school history teacher in Freeport, Illinois. He also coached basketball and wrestling. In 1930, he was hired as the Kentucky Wildcats' basketball coach. He was a tough leader and expected each player to work as hard as he could. It paid off: the Wildcats never had a losing season with Rupp. They won twenty-seven SEC championships, one NIT championship (in 1946, when the NIT was as prestigious as the NCAA tournament), and four NCAA championships (1948, 1949, 1951, 1958). Rupp was SEC Coach of the Year seven times and National Coach of the Year four times. On April 13, 1969, three years before he retired from coaching, Rupp was inducted into the Basketball Hall of Fame. To this day, among NCAA coaches with more than 500 wins, Rupp has the highest winning percentage of all time (.822).

After he left Kentucky, Rupp coached two professional teams. In 1976, the Wildcats' new arena was named Rupp Arena. Rupp passed away in 1977 at the age of seventy-six. Every year since 1972, the Adolph Rupp Trophy, named in his honor, is given to the best player in college basketball.

## C. M. Newton

Charles Martin Newton played guard and forward for Rupp's Kentucky Wildcats in the 1950s. He helped the team win a national championship in 1951. In 1956, Newton landed his first coaching job at Transylvania College in Lexington, Kentucky. In 1965, he recruited the school's first African American player.

After he proved his ability as a basketball coach, the University of Alabama hired Newton in 1968 to coach the Crimson Tide. In twelve seasons, he led the team to a record of 211–113. They won three straight SEC titles (1974, 1975, 1976). Just as he had at Transylvania, Newton recruited Alabama's first African American player, Wendell Hudson, in 1969.

In 1980, Newton retired from coaching and became an assistant commissioner for the SEC. However, in 1982, Vanderbilt University offered him the head coaching position with the Commodores. In eight seasons, Newton led the Commodores to a record of 129–115, and two NCAA tournament appearances. He also won SEC Coach of the Year in 1988 and 1989.

## Dale Brown

Dale Brown set many athletic records while in high school in Minot, North Dakota. He also excelled in basketball, football, and track during college, in the

Coach C. M. Newton speaks with forward Don Bowerman during a game in the 1976–1977 season.

## Reforming College Basketball

C. M. Newton had a successful career as a head coach, but he is also remembered for his contributions off the court. From 1979 to 1985, Newton was the chair of the NCAA Rules Committee. He helped shape the game to what is played today by advocating and establishing the three-point line, the shot clock, and the coach's box.

In 1989, Newton was hired to be the athletic director at the University of Kentucky. He helped to put together the historic 1992 team that UK fans named the Unforgettables. Newton also hired Kentucky's first male and female African American basketball coaches. When it comes to basketball, Newton certainly did it all—he was a player, coach, administrator, and reformer. Newton was inducted into the Basketball Hall of Fame in 2000 as a contributor to the sport of basketball.

Dale Brown, shown here during a game in 1991, was known as a vocal coach on and off the court. He was even an outspoken critic of the NCAA.

late 1950s. After college, Brown coached high school basketball. He was also briefly an assistant coach with Utah State University and Washington State University.

In 1972, Brown was hired as the head coach of the LSU basketball team. Some people told Brown he was making a mistake coaching basketball for LSU. He was the first coach to take the job after the well-liked coach Peter "Press" Maravich. Some said Kentucky was too dominant. Others said football was too popular in Louisiana for basketball to thrive. Brown set out to prove them wrong.

Brown traveled across the state, giving out basketball nets in LSU's colors of purple and gold and talking about the sport to anyone who would listen. He soon earned the respect and approval of LSU fans. Brown also worked hard to recruit the best players he could find. The LSU Tigers began to improve in the mid-1970s. In 1977, during the regular season, Brown led the Tigers to an exciting overtime win over a strong Kentucky Wildcats team.

During his twenty-five years as head coach, Brown led the Tigers to 448 wins, the most wins by any LSU basketball coach. In SEC wins, he is second only to Adolph Rupp. The Tigers won four regular season SEC championships (1979, 1981, 1986, 1991) and one SEC tournament (1980). They reached the Final Four in 1981 and 1986. The 1986 team became the first 11th-seed team to reach the Final Four. On their way to the Final Four, they defeated the number 1, 2, and 3 seeds—something many basketball experts had considered impossible. Brown was a four-time SEC Coach of the Year (1973, 1979, 1981, 1989) and National Coach of the Year in 1981. Although Brown never won a national championship with LSU, he is remembered as the man who put LSU basketball on the map.

## Orlando "Tubby" Smith

Orlando "Tubby" Smith got his first assistant coaching job with Virginia Commonwealth University in 1979. While he was there, he formed the foundation for his "ball-line defense," which has remained the basis for his coaching style to this day. Using this strategy, all defenders must stay between the line of the ball and the baseline. In 1986, Smith became an assistant coach with the South Carolina Gamecocks. In 1989, he joined the Kentucky Wildcats as an assistant coach under Rick Pitino. Thanks to great improvements in the Wildcats' record, Smith was promoted to associate coach.

Smith met with immediate success in his first head-coaching position at Oklahoma's Tulsa University from 1991 to 1995. In 1995, Smith became the first African American head coach of the Georgia Bulldogs. Although Smith stayed with the Bulldogs just two years, he left a lasting impression. The Bulldogs had back-to-back seasons of twenty or more wins for the first time in the school's history. With Smith as their leader, the Bulldogs made it into the NCAA tournament both years.

Orlando "Tubby" Smith directs the Georgia Bulldogs from the sidelines during a game against Georgia Tech in December 1995.

In 1997, Smith returned to the University of Kentucky, this time as head coach. He was their first African American head coach. In his first season, Smith coached the Wildcats to their seventh NCAA championship. The team was nicknamed the "Comeback Cats" for their ability to win after trailing for much of their games. In his nine seasons with Kentucky, Smith helped the Wildcats win five SEC championships (1998, 1999, 2001, 2003, 2005) and five SEC tournaments (1998, 1999, 2001, 2003, 2004). Smith reached 100 wins with Kentucky in 130 games. Only Adolph Rupp reached that mark more quickly. He is one of only five coaches to win 365 games in fifteen seasons or less.

Smith has won several coaching awards, including the Naismith College Coach of the Year Award in 2003 and the Jim Phelan Coach of the Year Award in 2005. Smith is now the head coach at the University of Minnesota. With 387 wins and 145 losses, he is currently the eighth most successful active coach.

# CHAPTER 3

# Key Players in the SEC

**Numerous** great basketball players got their start in the SEC. The players featured in this chapter are on the list of the 50 Greatest Players in NBA History. (This NBA list was voted on by a variety of players, coaches, and media personnel.) There are certainly many other talented and impressive SEC players, but these four are arguably among the best to ever play in the conference.

## "Pistol Pete" Maravich

Pete Maravich, nicknamed "Pistol Pete," is widely regarded as the best college basketball player of all time. Maravich grew up playing basketball. His father, "Press" Maravich, taught him the basics of the game at an early age. He had an amazing high school career, and his father—who at the time was head coach at LSU—convinced him to attend LSU.

"Pistol Pete" Maravich broke the all-time scoring record on January 31, 1979, during a home game in Baton Rouge, Louisiana. After the game was over, celebrating players and fans carried Maravich off the court. Press, Pete's father and coach, is among the crowd of onlookers.

Maravich played guard for the LSU Tigers from 1968 to 1970. In his first game, he scored fifty points. During his three years with the LSU varsity team, he scored 3,667 points, averaging an amazing 44.2 points per game. Maravich is still the all-time points leader in college basketball. He set eleven NCAA records, thirty-four SEC records, and every LSU record in points scored, scoring average, field goals attempted and made, free throws attempted and made, and assists. Although LSU never won a championship while Maravich played for them, he helped turn a losing team into a true contender.

Maravich was the National Player of the Year in 1969 and 1970. He won the Naismith Award in 1970. He went on to a memorable career in the NBA and was a six-time NBA All-Star. After ten years in the NBA, Maravich retired due to a leg injury. He became the youngest person to be inducted into the Basketball Hall of Fame in 1987. Tragically, Maravich suffered a fatal heart attack while playing basketball with friends in 1988. It was caused by a rare heart defect.

## Dominique Wilkins

Dominique Wilkins played forward for the Georgia Bulldogs from 1980 to 1982. To this day, he is the only Georgia

Dominique Wilkins slam-dunks the ball during a March 1981 game against LSU.

player to have had his jersey retired. An electric player with the nickname of "the Human Highlight Film," Wilkins is remembered for his dominating offensive game, especially his stunning ability to slam-dunk the ball. He continually wowed crowds with his amazing leaps and dunks. He led the Bulldogs in scoring three straight years and averaged 21.6 points a game. He still holds the Georgia records for most points scored in a season (732) and field goals (723).

In the NBA, Wilkins played for the Atlanta Hawks, Los Angeles Clippers, Boston Celtics, San Antonio Spurs, and Orlando Magic. Wilkins was the 1985–1986 NBA scoring champ, with an average of 30.3 points a game. He was a nine-time NBA All-Star and won two NBA slam dunk contests (in 1985 and 1990). Wilkins was

## SEC Award Winners

The following is a list of SEC athletes and coaches who have won national awards. Many other awards are given away each year, but the following are some of the most prestigious.

**Naismith Men's College Player of the Year Award (awarded since 1969)**
Pete Maravich, LSU, 1970

**Adolph Rupp Trophy (College Player of the Year Award, awarded since 1972)**
Shaquille O'Neal, LSU, 1991

**Oscar Robertson Trophy (College Player of the Year Award, awarded since 1959)**
Pete Maravich, LSU, 1969
Pete Maravich, LSU, 1970

**NCAA Basketball Tournament Most Outstanding Player (awarded since 1939)**
Alex Groza, Kentucky, 1948
Alex Groza, Kentucky, 1949
Bill Spivey, Kentucky, 1951
Jack Givens, Kentucky, 1978
Corliss Williamson, Arkansas, 1994
Tony Delk, Kentucky, 1996
Jeff Sheppard, Kentucky, 1998
Joakim Noah, Florida, 2006
Corey Brewer, Florida, 2007

**Naismith Men's College Coach of the Year Award (awarded since 1987)**
Nolan Richardson, Arkansas, 1994
Rod Barnes, Ole Miss, 2001
Orlando "Tubby" Smith, Kentucky, 2003

**Henry Iba Coach of the Year Award (awarded since 1959)**
Adolph Rupp, Kentucky, 1966
Eddie Sutton, Arkansas, 1977
Eddie Fogler, Vanderbilt, 1993
Cliff Ellis, Auburn, 1999
Orlando "Tubby" Smith, Kentucky, 2003

inducted into the Georgia Sports Hall of Fame in 2004 and the Basketball Hall of Fame in 2006.

## Charles Barkley

Charles Barkley played power forward for Auburn University in the early 1980s. Despite the fact that at times he weighed close to 300 pounds (136 kilograms), Barkley amazed crowds with his athletic ability. He excelled at dunking the ball and blocking shots. He also led the SEC in rebounds for three years straight. Due to his size and ability, he earned the nickname "the

Charles Barkley uses his height to his advantage as he dunks a field goal during a regular season game against Alabama, circa 1981–1984.

Round Mound of Rebound." Barkley was SEC Player of the Year in 1984. He holds school records for field-goal percentage (.626) and blocks (145). The *Birmingham Post Herald* named him the SEC Player of the Decade.

Barkley left Auburn after his junior year to join the NBA. For sixteen years he was one of the NBA's most dominant players. In 1992 and 1996, he won Olympic gold medals with the U.S. men's basketball team. Barkley's Auburn jersey was retired in 2003. In 2006, he was inducted into the Basketball Hall of Fame.

Shaquille O'Neal slam-dunks the ball during an NCAA tournament game against the Southeastern Louisiana University Lions in 1991. That season, which was Shaq's sophomore year, O'Neal was voted college basketball's National Player of the Year.

# Shaquille O'Neal

At 7 feet, 1 inch (2.13 meters), and 325 pounds (147 kg), Shaquille O'Neal—known as Shaq—is one of the most imposing players in the game of basketball today. O'Neal began playing center for LSU in 1989. In 1991, the Tigers were SEC champions. That year, O'Neal was voted National Player of the Year. He was a two-time SEC Player of the Year (1991, 1992). He also received the Adolph Rupp Trophy in 1991. O'Neal is fourth on LSU's list of all-time scorers with 1,941 points. He currently holds the NCAA record for shots blocked in a single game (17).

O'Neal is the youngest and only active player of the 50 Greatest Players in NBA History. He has won the NBA championship four times—three with the Los Angeles Lakers and once with the Miami Heat—and was MVP (Most Valuable Player) three times. After fifteen years in the pros, Shaq is truly in a league of his own. By the end of the 2006–2007 season, he had more than 25,000 points and over 10,000 rebounds! In 2000, O'Neal was inducted into the LSU Hall of Fame. There's no doubt that he will one day be in the Basketball Hall of Fame as well.

# Key Games in the SEC

**Prior** to the regular season conference games, SEC teams play about thirteen to sixteen games against teams from other conferences. These games are played in November and December. Starting in early January, they then play sixteen games within the conference. Each team plays the other teams in their division twice—once at home and once away. They also play the teams from the other division once during the regular season.

The SEC team with the best record at the end of the regular season is declared the SEC champion. Kentucky has won a stunning forty-three SEC championships. LSU is in distant second with nine. Only one SEC team—the Ole Miss Rebels—has yet to win a championship. Since the Kentucky Wildcats are most often the team to beat, they are involved in most of the traditional SEC rivalries. Arkansas and Kentucky—historically the top two teams in the SEC (especially

Mississippi State point guard Jamont Gordon sprints by three Alabama players on his way to the hoop. As a sophomore during the 2006–2007 season, Gordon led the Bulldogs in scoring, rebounds, and assists.

in the 1990s)—have had the most heated competitions. Kentucky is also considered a rival to Florida and Tennessee. Other SEC rivalries include Alabama and Mississippi State, and Tennessee and Florida.

## The SEC Tournament and Championship

The results at the end of the regular season decide which teams play each other in the SEC tournament. This is a single-elimination

Several players from Kentucky and Alabama battle it out for a rebound during a heated SEC Conference tournament game in March 2006.

tournament; if a team loses once, it is out of the tournament. The top teams in the East and West Divisions each receive a bye for the first round, which means that they do not compete until the second round. The SEC tournament is designed so that the top teams from both divisions will be matched up in the final round of the tournament. However, this rarely actually happens since competition is fierce and there are often upsets. The team that wins the tournament is crowned SEC Tournament Champion and receives an automatic bid for the NCAA tournament.

Other SEC teams can make it into the NCAA tournament based on their regular season records.

As in the regular season, the Kentucky Wildcats have traditionally dominated the SEC tournament. In fact, they have won so many SEC tournament games that the tournament is sometimes referred to as the Wildcat Invitational. The Wildcats have won twenty-five of the forty-eight tournaments that have been played so far. Alabama has won the second-most titles, with six.

# The NCAA Tournament

Since the first postseason competition in 1939, the NCAA basketball tournament has featured classic matchups, exciting upsets, and stunning victories. Commonly known as March Madness or the Big Dance, it is one of the most popular athletic showdowns in the United States. Of the 336 Division I NCAA basketball teams, only the top sixty-five make it to the tournament each year. The top team from each conference automatically qualifies. An NCAA selection committee then chooses the rest of the teams based on their win-loss records and rankings. The teams are organized into four regions (East, South, West, and Midwest) based on where that leg of the tournament takes place. The two lowest-ranked teams play the first game to see which team will enter the tournament.

The SEC usually has several teams in the tournament and often does very well in its standings. Five SEC teams competed in the 2007 NCAA tournament: Arkansas, Florida, Kentucky, Tennessee, and Vanderbilt. Tennessee, Vanderbilt, and Florida made it to the Sweet Sixteen. Florida won the final game and became the 2007 champion.

With forty-nine appearances, the Kentucky Wildcats have an especially impressive record in the NCAA tournament. The most exciting season for the Wildcats may well have been 1996–1997. The team was undefeated, earning the nickname "The Untouchables." They won the 1997 national championship and went down in the record books as one of the most successful college basketball teams of all time.

# NCAA National Championship

The NCAA tournament concludes with much fanfare and excitement as the best teams from the four regions battle it out in the Final

Four. The winner of the Final Four is declared the year's national champion. The team receives both the gold-plated NCAA National Championship Trophy and the more elaborate Siemens Trophy, a Waterford crystal basketball.

SEC teams have had their share of victories, but they've also suffered some stunning upsets. In a game widely believed to be the best college basketball game ever played, the Kentucky Wildcats lost to the Duke Blue Devils in the 1992 East regional championship game. In a remarkable attempt to extend their season, the Wildcats fought back from a seventeen-point deficit. Late in overtime, Kentucky was ahead 103–102, and the Wildcats thought they had the victory. However, with two seconds left, Blue Devil Grant Hill threw a seventy-five-foot pass to Christian Laettner. He sank a seventeen-foot jump shot—just as the buzzer sounded to end the game, 104–103.

## What Is the NIT?

The NCAA tournament is not the only annual college basketball tournament. The National Invitation Tournament (NIT) was founded in 1938. It originally consisted of six teams, but it expanded gradually over the years, until it had forty teams in 2002. In 2007, the number of teams was decreased to thirty-two.

The NIT is actually made up of two separate contests. The NIT Season Tip-Off is a preseason tournament held in November. This competition was founded in 1985 and usually features sixteen teams that had successful seasons the previous year. The postseason NIT takes place in March, featuring the best teams that didn't make it to the NCAA tournament. The final rounds take place at Madison Square Garden in New York City. The NIT was once as important as the NCAA tournament. Today, however, it is known as a competition for teams that failed to make the NCAA tournament.

Members of the Florida Gators celebrate their first national title on April 3, 2006, after defeating the UCLA Bruins at the RCA Dome in Indianapolis, Indiana. Freshman guard Walter Hodge holds the trophy, appreciating the moment and the crowd with his teammates.

## Florida Gators: Reigning Champions

The Kentucky Wildcats have seven national titles (only the Pac-10 Conference's UCLA has more, with eleven). Three other SEC teams have won a national championship: Florida has won two, and Arkansas and LSU have each won one. The biggest SEC story lately, however, is the Florida Gators and their back-to-back 2006 and 2007 national championships. The Gators achieved this feat with the same starting lineup—Corey Brewer, Taurean Green, Al Horford,

Lee Humphrey, and Joakim Noah. During the 2005–2006 season, this talented squad led the Gators to a 27–6 record, including a seventeen-game winning streak. The Gators went on to win the NCAA championship game against UCLA. Forward Joakim Noah was named tournament MVP.

The Gators ended their 2006–2007 season 26–5, then won their third straight SEC tournament championship. On March 31, 2007, the team once again beat the UCLA Bruins, this time during a Final Four battle. The Gators met another basketball powerhouse, the Ohio State Buckeyes, in the NCAA championship game. In beating the Buckeyes 84–75, the Gators became the first college basketball team since 1992 to win back-to-back championships. The team is also the first to win with the same lineup two years in a row. Forward Corey Brewer was named the MVP, and head coach Billy Donovan became the twelfth coach ever to win multiple NCAA championships.

## The Future Is Bright

The Gators' win drew even more attention to the SEC. Several NBA teams wanted to hire Donovan as their head coach. He signed with the Orlando Magic, but five days later, he had second thoughts and decided instead to return as head coach of the Gators.

Many fans wonder if Donovan and the Gators will be able to make history by winning a third straight NCAA championship. Some are eager to see if another competitive SEC team, such as South Carolina, Tennessee, or Vanderbilt, can rise up and claim the title of champion. Whatever happens, with its long history of success, the SEC is sure to continue to be a college basketball leader.

# Mascots in the SEC

**While** college mascots may be most remembered for their presence at football games, they also play an important role on the basketball court. College mascots are symbols that have come to be cherished by fans. Costumed mascots help get the crowd cheering for their team and entertain fans with their energetic routines. The mascots of the SEC have a special place in the hearts of college basketball fans.

## Albert and Alberta

Since 1907, the alligator has been the symbol of the University of Florida athletic teams. In 1957, the first of several live alligator mascots took up residence at the university in Gainesville, Florida.

In 1970, the University of Florida added its first costumed mascot to the team—Albert E. Gator. Albert was joined by Alberta

Albert E. Gator cheers on the Florida Gators during a first-round game of the 2003 NCAA tournament.

in 1986. Albert and Alberta entertain fans at home games at the Gators' O'Connell Center.

## Uga, the Georgia Bulldog

The University of Georgia mascot, Uga the English bulldog, is perhaps the most recognizable mascot in college athletics. There have been six bulldogs named Uga since 1955, when Georgia began its tradition of having a live mascot. Uga has been kidnapped by opposing teams several times, has been photographed with politicians, and has appeared on the cover of *Sports Illustrated*. The fifth Uga even appeared in the movie *Midnight in the Garden of Good and Evil*! Uga attends Georgia home basketball games. The team also has a costumed mascot named Hairy Dog, who attends home games.

## Wildcat, Scratch, and Blue

Two costumed mascots, Wildcat and Scratch, join the Kentucky Wildcats at all home basketball games held at Rupp Arena in Lexington, Kentucky. Wildcat first appeared during the 1976–1977

Wildcat entertains fans by gliding across the court at the Louisiana Superdome during a 2003 NCAA tournament game against Vanderbilt University. Kentucky beat Vanderbilt 81–63.

season. Scratch is a mascot who especially entertains kids and is the host of UK's official Kids Club.

The Kentucky athletic program also has a live mascot: a bobcat named Blue. Blue does not attend games because bobcats, also called wildcats, are very shy and do not like large crowds. Blue can be visited at Salato Wildlife Education Center, near Frankfort, Kentucky.

## Cocky

Cocky is the mascot of the South Carolina Fighting Gamecocks. A gamecock is a strong, fighting rooster. The state of South Carolina was known for the breeding and training of fighting gamecocks. Although in the United States gamecocks were once widely used to stage cockfights, today, raising fighting birds and cockfighting are illegal in almost every state.

Cocky, a costumed mascot, has been entertaining fans for twenty-eight years. He took over for his "father," Big Spur, in 1980. Cocky attends all home and away Gamecock basketball games.

## Smokey

In 1953, students at the University of Tennessee decided they wanted a live mascot. As a result, at halftime during a football game against Mississippi State, a number of bluetick coonhounds were lined up in front of the hometown crowd. When Smokey's name was announced, the dog barked! The crowd responded with cheers, which made Smokey howl even louder. Smokey was thus chosen to be Tennessee's mascot. Since 1953, there have been nine Bluetick Coonhounds named Smokey. Tennessee also has a costumed mascot named Smokey, who entertains fans during home basketball games.

## Mr. C

Cornelius Vanderbilt, the founder of Vanderbilt University, was a shipping magnate. His nickname was "Commodore," although he wasn't really in the navy. Vanderbilt's mascot, Mr. C, was named after the university's founder. He resembles a nineteenth-century naval commander. Mr. C is a familiar sight at Vanderbilt home basketball games and at basketball tournaments.

## Big Al

The Alabama University sports teams have long been known as the Crimson Tide. This name came from a football game played against Auburn in 1948. The two teams played on a field of red mud, and Alabama won. Since 1930, however, the Alabama mascot has been an elephant. (In an article after one of its football games, a sports writer described the Alabama team as a pack of elephants, and their mascot was born.) Big Al, the Crimson Tide mascot, can be found at every home Alabama basketball game, entertaining fans and leading them in cheers.

Big Al storms down the side of the court during a home game at Coleman Coliseum in Tuscaloosa, Alabama.

## Mike the Tiger

The LSU Tigers have one of the most intimidating mascots in all of college sports: a live Bengal tiger named Mike. Although Mike is mainly associated with LSU football, he does make the occasional appearance with the basketball team. In 1991, Mike accompanied

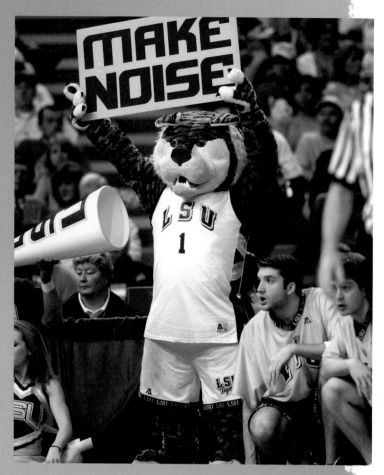

Mike the Tiger leads LSU fans in cheers during a 2003 NCAA tournament game in the Louisiana Superdome.

Shaquille O'Neal and the rest of the LSU basketball team to the Louisiana Superdome. There, he watched LSU beat the Texas Longhorns 84–83. Mike was the fifth Bengal tiger to represent the team. Unfortunately, he passed away in May 2007. LSU is hoping to have another Mike the Tiger by the start of the 2008 football season.

LSU also has a costumed Mike the Tiger, who can be seen at LSU basketball games at LSU's Pete Maravich Assembly Center.

## Colonel Reb

The Ole Miss Rebels currently do not have an on-field mascot. However, most Rebel fans have remained supporters of Colonel Reb, who was the mascot from 1979 to 2003. Many think that Colonel Reb, dressed as a southern gentleman with a red suit, red hat, and white hair, is patterned after a man named Blind Jim Ivy. Jim Ivy had been a dedicated fan of the Rebels up until he died in 1955. Other people, particularly school administrators, feared that Colonel Reb could be interpreted as a symbol of slavery in the "Old South." Ole Miss is still searching for a new mascot. Die-hard fans would prefer that Colonel Reb return to the Rebels' games.

## Aubie and Nova

The Auburn sports teams are known as the Auburn Tigers, but some people mistakenly call them the Auburn War Eagles. This is because they are represented by two mascots—Aubie the Tiger and Nova the Golden Eagle. Nova is a live eagle that appears only at home football games. Aubie is a costumed mascot who appears at football and basketball games. He first appeared in 1958, as a cartoon character on Auburn game programs. In 1979, Aubie became a costumed mascot and made his first appearances at Auburn basketball games. Aubie has won six national mascot championships, more than any other mascot in the country.

### What's Next for Ole Miss?

The University of Mississippi has worked to distance itself from the Confederate flag and other images that have come to symbolize the Old South. Many people feel these images are racist, although others honor them as important southern traditions. Colonel Reb is another symbol Ole Miss has tried to eliminate from the school. In 2003, the administration held a contest to select a new mascot. However, fans rejected all of the suggestions.

Many Ole Miss fans are still trying to bring back Colonel Reb. The Colonel Reb Foundation (CRF) is the most vocal of the groups. It has created a new mascot, Colonel Too, to take Colonel Reb's place. The school, however, does not sanction this mascot and even makes him pay for a ticket to every game he attends. The CRF plans to keep Colonel Too around until Colonel Reb is allowed to return to the Ole Miss sidelines.

Big Red performs for fans during a 2007 NCAA tournament game between the Razorbacks and the USC Trojans.

# A "Wild Band of Razorback Hogs!"

After a win against LSU in 1909, Arkansas football coach Hugo Bezdek said that his team had played like a "wild band of razorback hogs." The name "Razorbacks" stuck.

Arkansas may have the most mascots of any college team. Tusk is a live Russian boar who lives on a nearby farm. Big Red is a costumed razorback and the leader of the Arkansas mascots. Sue E. is a female razorback mascot. Other mascots include Pork Chop, a favorite with the kids, and Boss Hog, who, when inflated, is nine feet tall (2.74 meters).

# GLOSSARY

**assist**  An act by a player that enables a teammate to score.

**center**  The player in basketball who is usually the tallest and strongest player on the team, and who is expected to make big plays close to the net.

**coach's box**  The area next to the court where the coach is allowed to stand during a game.

**commodore**  An officer in the navy.

**contender**  A competitor, especially someone who has a good chance to win.

**controversial**  Causing disagreement between people.

**dominant**  In control or command over others.

**feat**  A remarkable act or achievement.

**field goal**  In basketball, when the ball enters the basket for two or three points. This does not include free throws.

**forward**  One of two players on a basketball team that plays in the corners and scores points.

**free throw**  The chance to shoot a basket without the other team trying to stop you. Free throws are awarded to a player who has been fouled.

**guard**  One of two players on a basketball team who plays in the backcourt. Guards usually set up plays and make passes to players closer to the net.

**initiate**  To cause something to begin.

**magnate**  Someone in business or industry who has a lot of wealth and power.

**overtime**  An extra period added to a basketball game when the score is tied at the end of regulation play.

**power forward**  A forward who is bigger and stronger than other forwards, and who is likely to be better at close shots, blocking shots, and rebounds.

**premier**  First in rank, position, or importance.

**rebound**  Recovery of the ball after it bounces off the backboard or rim of the basket.

**recruit**  To get someone to join a team or other group.

**reigning**  In power; the current champion.

**rival**  A person or group against whom one regularly competes.

**sanction**  Official permission or approval for a course of action.

**seed**  In basketball, the ranking a team receives at the beginning of a tournament, based on the likelihood that they will win the tournament.

**shot clock**  A clock used in basketball to limit the time a team may take before shooting the ball.

**Sweet Sixteen**  In basketball, the final sixteen teams left in a tournament.

**three-point shot**  A field goal that is taken from behind the three-point line and is worth three points.

# FOR MORE INFORMATION

International Basketball Federation (FIBA)
Avenue Louis Casaï, 53
1216 Cointrin, Geneva
Switzerland
Web site: http://www.fiba.com
An association of national organizations that defines the international rules of basketball and govern international competition.

Naismith Memorial Basketball
  Hall of Fame
1000 West Columbus Avenue
Springfield, MA 01105
(877) 4HOOPLA (446-6752)
(413) 781-6500
Web site: http://www.hoophall.com
The Naismith Memorial Basketball Hall of Fame honors basketball's greatest players, coaches, contributors, referees, and teams.

National Association of Basketball
  Coaches (NABC)
1111 Main Street, Suite 1000
Kansas City, MO 64105-2136
(816) 878-NABC (6222)
Web site: http://nabc.cstv.com
Founded by Phog Allen in 1927, this association aims to educate the public regarding the connection between coaches and students/players, develop the rules of the game, and honor the sport's great coaches.

The National Collegiate Athletic Association (NCAA)
700 W. Washington Street
P.O. Box 6222
Indianapolis, IN 46206-6222
(317) 917-6222
Web site: http://www.ncaa.org
The NCAA is the largest college athletics association in the United States. It is made up of approximately 1,200 institutions, organizations, conferences, and individuals.

Southeastern Conference
2201 Richard Arrington Boulevard North
Birmingham, AL 35203
(205) 458-3000
Web site: http://www.secsports.com
The official headquarters of the Southeastern Conference. The conference's Web site offers a wealth of information about member schools and teams.

## Web Sites

Due to the changing nature of Internet links, Rosen Publishing has developed an online list of Web sites related to the subject of this book. This site is updated regularly. Please use this link to access the list:

http://www.rosenlinks.com/imcb/bsec

# FOR FURTHER READING

Baker, David G., and Margaret Taylor Stewart. *Tales of Mike the Tiger: Facts And Fun for Everyone*. Baton Rouge, LA: Louisiana State University Press, 2006.

DeCock, Luke. *Great Teams in College Basketball History* (Great Teams). Chicago, IL: Raintree, 2006.

Macnow, Glen. *Charles Barkley* (Sports Great). Rev. ed. Berkeley Heights, NJ: Enslow Publishers, 1998.

NCAA. *NCAA March Madness: Cinderellas, Superstars, and Champions from the NCAA Final Four*. Chicago, IL: Triumph Books, 2004.

Robinson, Tom. *Shaquille O'Neal: Giant On and Off the Court* (Sports Stars with Heart). Berkeley Heights, NJ: Enslow Publishers, 2006.

Sachare, Alex. *The Basketball Hall of Fame Hoop Facts & Stats*. New York, NY: John Wiley & Sons, Inc., 1998.

Stewart, Mark. *Basketball: A History of Hoops* (The Watts History of Sports). Danbury, CT: Franklin Watts, 1999.

Stewart, Mark. *The Final Four* (The Watts History of Sports). Danbury, CT: Franklin Watts, 2002.

Sullivan, George. *All About Basketball*. New York, NY: G.P. Putnam's Sons, 1991.

Thomas, Keltie. *How Basketball Works*. Toronto, ON: Maple Tree Press, 2005.

# BIBLIOGRAPHY

Dortch, Chris. *String Music: Inside the Rise of SEC Basketball*. Dulles, VA: Brassey's, Inc., 2002.

Forde, Pat. "'92 Loss to Duke Proved UK Could Win Again." ESPN.com. December 17, 2001. Retrieved May 31, 2007 (http://espn.go.com/ncb/columns/forde_pat/1297334.html).

Gatorzone.com. "Men's Basketball Captures Back-to-Back National Championships." April 3, 2007. Retrieved May 31, 2007 (http://www.gatorzone.com/story.php?game_id=6787&sport=baskm).

NIT.org. "NIT History." Retrieved May 30, 2007 (http://www.nit.org/history/nit-history.html).

NIT.org. "NIT Season Tip-Off/Preseason NIT Overview." Retrieved May 30, 2007 (http://www.nit.org/history/nit-preseason.html).

Pells, Eddie. "(11) Florida 73, (7) UCLA 57." Yahoo! Sports. April 4, 2006. Retrieved June 1, 2007 (http://sports.yahoo.com/ncaab/recap?gid=200604030606).

Pells, Eddie. "(1) Florida 84, (1) Ohio St. 75." Yahoo! Sports. April 3, 2007. Retrieved June 1, 2007 (http://sports.yahoo.com/ncaab/recap?gid=200704020210).

SECsports.com. "Through the Years." Retrieved May 30, 2007 (http://www.secsports.com/doc_lib/bkc_through_the_years.pdf ).

SECsports.com. "2006–07 SEC Men's Basketball Year in Review." May 3, 2007. Retrieved May 25, 2007 (http://www.secsports.com/index.php?url_channel_id=3&url_subchannel_id=&url_article_id=8926&change_well_id=2).

Warner, Chris. *SEC Basketball History & Tradition* (Traditions of the SEC). Baton Rouge, LA: CEW Enterprises, 2001.

Warner, Chris. *A Tailgater's Guide to SEC Football* (Traditions of the SEC). Baton Rouge, LA: CEW Enterprises, 2004.

# INDEX

## About the Author

Greg Roza is a writer and editor who specializes in creating library books and educational materials. He lives in Hamburg, New York, with his wife, Abigail; son, Lincoln; and daughters, Autumn and Daisy. Roza has a master's degree in English from SUNY Fredonia and loves to stay in shape by participating in athletic activities. He has written a number of books for Rosen, including Football in the *SEC (Southeastern Conference)* and *Paintball: Rules, Tips, Strategy, and Safety*.

## Photo Credits

Cover (top), pp. 16, 24, 28, 34, 35, 38, 40 © Getty Images; cover (bottom) © Jim Burgess; p. 1 © www.stockphoto.com/Luis Lotax; p. 3 (left) © www.istockphoto.com/Benjamin Goode; pp. 4–5, 18 © University of Georgia; pp. 3 (right) 6, 12, 19, 26, 33 © www.istockphoto.com; pp. 7, 13, 20 © AP Photos; pp. 8, 15, 22, 30, 39 © www.istockphoto.com/Bill Grove; p. 9 © The Granger Collection; pp. 15, 37 © University of Alabama; p. 21 © Terry Allen; p. 23 © Collegiate Images; p. 27 © Mississippi State University; p. 31 © University of Florida.

**Designer:** Tom Forget
**Photo Researcher:** Marty Levick